DISCARDED
SOUTH RUTLAND ELEMENTARY

SOUTH RUTLAND
ELEMENTARY LIBRARY

Afghanistan

Many Cultures, One World

by Barbara Knox

Consultant:
Khairya Y. Sammander
Afghan Community Foundation
Atlanta, Georgia

Blue Earth Books
an imprint of Capstone Press
Mankato, Minnesota

Blue Earth Books are published by Capstone Press
151 Good Counsel Drive, P.O. Box 669, Mankato, Minnesota 56002
http://www.capstonepress.com

Copyright © 2004 by Capstone Press. All rights reserved.

No part of this book may be reproduced in whole or in part, or stored in a retrieval system, or transmitted in any form
or by any means, electronic, mechanical, photocopying, recording, or otherwise, without written permission from the publisher.
For information regarding permission, write to Capstone Press, 151 Good Counsel Drive,
P.O. Box 669, Dept. R, Mankato, Minnesota 56002.
Printed in the United States of America

Library of Congress Cataloging-in-Publication Data
Knox, Barbara.
    Afghanistan / by Barbara Knox.
    p. cm.—(Many cultures, one world)
    Includes bibliographical references and index.
    Contents: About Afghanistan—An Afghan legend—City and country life—Seasons in Afghanistan—Family life in Afghanistan—Laws,
rules, and customs—Pets in Afghanistan—Sights to see in Afghanistan.
    ISBN 0-7368-2448-0 (hardcover)
    1. Afghanistan—Juvenile literature. [1. Afghanistan.] I. Title. II. Series.
DS351.5.K56 2004
958.1—dc22
                                                                 2003017176

Editorial credits
Editor: Megan Schoeneberger
Series Designer: Kia Adams
Photo Researcher: Alta Schaffer
Product Planning Editor: Eric Kudalis

Cover photo
The Blue Mosque in Mazar-e Sharif, Afghanistan,
by Victor Englebert

Artistic effects
PhotoDisc Inc.

Photo credits
Capstone Press/Gary Sundermeyer, 3 (necklace, drink), 21, 25,
    back cover
Courtesy of Gayle Zonnefeld, 23 (bottom right)
Corbis/AFP, 22, 23 (left), 24; Baci, 20; Michael S. Yamashita, 10, 19 (right);
    Reuters NewMedia Inc., 6, 13 (right), 16–17; Reza/Webistan, 28–29;
    Roger Wood, 9 (right); Setboun, 14; Yann Arthus-Bertrand,
    27 (right)
Corbis Sygma/Silva Joao, 11
Getty Images Inc./Ami Vitale, 8–9
John Elk III, 29 (right)
One Mile Up Inc., 23 (top right)
PhotoDisc Inc., 3 (marbles), 15
SuperStock/George Hunter, 26–27
TRIP/C. Watmough, 12–13; R. Zampese, 17 (right), 18–19;
    Steve Maines, 4–5

1 2 3 4 5 6 09 08 07 06 05 04

Chapter 1
About Afghanistan 4

Chapter 2
An Afghan Legend 8

Chapter 3
City and Country Life 12

Chapter 4
Seasons in Afghanistan 16

Chapter 5
Family Life in Afghanistan 18

Chapter 6
Laws, Rules, and Customs 22

Chapter 7
Pets in Afghanistan 26

Chapter 8
Sights to See in Afghanistan 28

Glossary 30
Read More 30
Useful Addresses 31
Internet Sites 31
Index 32

Turn to page 7 to find a map of Afghanistan.

Look on page 15 to learn a game many Afghan children play.

Check out page 21 to find out how to make an Afghan treat.

CHAPTER 1

About Afghanistan

Afghanistan's Hindu Kush Mountains have some of the tallest peaks in the world. They cover nearly two-thirds of Afghanistan.

Hindu Kush means "killer of Hindus." Many people have died trying to cross these mountains. The Khyber Pass is the main route through the mountains between Afghanistan and Pakistan.

The Hindu Kush Mountains stretch across most of Afghanistan. Clear lakes can be found in some parts of the mountains.

Facts about Afghanistan

Name: Afghanistan
Capital: Kabul
Population: About 27 million people
Size: 250,000 square miles (647,500 square kilometers)
Languages: Pashtu, Afghan Persian (Dari), Uzbek, Turkmen
Religions: Islamic (99 percent), other (1 percent)
Highest point: Nowshak, 24,557 feet (7,485 meters) above sea level
Lowest point: Amu River, 846 feet (258 meters) above sea level
Main crops: Wheat, fruit, nuts
Money: Afghani

A large desert stretches across southwestern Afghanistan. The desert is one of the driest deserts in the world. Afghans sometimes call it the "Desert of Death."

Afghanistan is a landlocked country about the size of Texas. It does not border any oceans or seas. Turkmenistan, Uzbekistan, and Tajikistan lie to the north.

Afghanistan also shares a short border with China. Pakistan wraps around the east and south. Iran is to the west.

Some Afghans live in the desert. They use camels to carry loads. Camels can go for many days without much water.

CHAPTER 2

An Afghan Legend

One thousand years ago, Afghanistan was part of a trade route. Traders passed through Afghanistan looking for treasure. Stories of their adventures were told year after year.

The people of Afghanistan still tell traditional stories. These legends date back hundreds or even thousands of years. Afghan legends are stories of magic and treasure.

Children laugh as a storyteller acts out a traditional legend.

The Khyber Pass is the major route between Afghanistan and Pakistan. For many years, traders used the path to pass through Afghanistan.

The Necklace of Life

Once upon a time, a farmer and his wife had a baby girl. The farmer did not want a daughter. He wanted only sons to help in the fields. He told his wife to kill the daughter.

The farmer's wife could not kill her own daughter. She hid the baby girl in a dark basement. The girl grew pale and sick.

One day, four fairies each gave the girl a gift. One fairy gave her the Necklace of Life. With the necklace, the girl would always be healthy.

The second fairy gave the girl laughter that made flowers fall at her feet. The third fairy gave the girl the power to cry tears of emeralds. The last fairy cast a spell so the ground turned into bricks of gold wherever the girl walked.

When the girl was older, the farmer's wife told a king about her daughter. The mother hired another woman to take the girl to the king. Instead, this woman hid the girl and put the Necklace of Life on her own daughter.

Farming in Afghanistan's dry soil is difficult work. Sons learn how to help their fathers with the work.

The king and his son were not fooled. The other girl could not cry tears of emeralds. Gold bricks did not appear where she stepped.

The king and his son searched for the real daughter. They found her hiding in an empty castle. Without the Necklace of Life, she had fallen into a deep sleep. The prince kissed her and she awoke. The prince put the Necklace of Life around her neck. She felt strong again. The farmer's daughter married the prince. They lived happily ever after, with many flowers, emeralds, and bricks of gold.

Afghans sell emeralds and other gems to people across the world. Gems are mined in the mountains of Afghanistan.

CHAPTER 3

City and Country Life

Most Afghans live in small villages. Many never travel beyond their own towns. They grow rice, vegetables, and wheat. Outdoor markets sell fruit, meat, and bread.

In these villages, people live much like they did 100 years ago. They have no running water or electricity. Most families do not have cars. Children walk to school. People use donkeys to carry heavy loads.

In small villages, people sell bananas, melons, and other food at stands in outdoor markets.

A boy rides a donkey carrying containers to fill with water from a well.

Some Afghans travel across the country with camels. These people are called **nomads**. Nomads live in tents and carry everything they own with them. They move from place to place to find food for their animals.

Few Afghans live in cities. Recent wars have wrecked many buildings. Many people escaped to nearby countries. Some families are returning. Many bring back TVs, radios, and other modern items.

Bombs have destroyed buildings in Kandahar and other cities. Afghans are now returning to rebuild their cities.

Bojol Baazi

Bojol baazi, or anklebone game, is a game for two players. Children in Afghanistan play this game with the anklebones of sheep. They collect the anklebones whenever their parents buy lamb meat. You can play this game using marbles. Afghan children also play other games using marbles.

What You Need

sidewalk or other outdoor surface
chalk
several marbles

What You Do

1. Draw a large chalk circle on the sidewalk.
2. Draw a straight line through the center of the circle, from one side to another. This line is the circle's diameter.
3. Both players line up the same number of marbles on the diameter line.
4. From outside the circle, players take turns rolling a marble to hit other marbles outside the circle. Players collect any marbles they knock out.
5. When all marbles have been knocked outside of the circle, the player who has collected the most marbles wins.

CHAPTER 4

Seasons in Afghanistan

Afghanistan's seasons range from icy cold to fiercely hot. In the mountains, winter is cold and snow falls. During summer, the desert is hot and dry.

Instead of rainstorms, the Afghan desert has sandstorms. Strong winds blow sand into clouds that swirl across the land. During sandstorms, people cannot see their hands held out in front of their faces.

Every spring, Afghans celebrate Now Ruz. This festival marks the first day of spring. It is the first day of the new year in Afghanistan.

A girl walks through a sandstorm. People cannot see very well when wind blows sand into the air.

Birthdays

Afghan children do not keep track of their birthdays. Families are too poor to spend money on birthdays. Many children do not even know the day they were born. They know only the season in which they were born.

Afghan families honor a new baby seven days after it is born. On the sixth day, the family names the child. Friends and family members bring gifts.

CHAPTER 5

Family Life in Afghanistan

Afghan culture separates men and women. Men lead their families. They make the most important decisions. Women cook, clean, and care for children.

Children do many chores to help the family. In the morning, they often walk to the town well for water. From the well, they carry water back to their home. They sometimes collect cow **dung** from the fields. They bring it home to dry. Families use the dried dung as fuel for their cooking fires.

Afghan men are in charge of their families. They make important decisions for the family.

Children carry large baskets filled with dung they have collected in the fields. The dung will be used for fuel.

People wash their hands very carefully before a meal. Instead of silverware, they use the fingers of their right hand to eat. They also use pieces of flat bread to scoop food into their mouths. Afghan families eat rice and bread with almost every meal.

Afghans are known for their kindness to strangers. Even poor families will give food and drinks to visitors. They offer sugared almonds, **pastries**, and sweet **cardamom** tea as special treats for guests.

A girl carries large pieces of flat bread called naan. Afghans eat this bread with most meals.

Raisin Drink

On hot days, children enjoy a special raisin drink. They pour the juice and raisins into a glass. They drink the juice and eat the raisins with a spoon. This sweet drink is simple to make.

What You Need

Ingredients
2 cups (480 mL) golden or dark raisins
water

Equipment
dry-ingredient measuring cup
glass bowl
plastic wrap
soup ladle
2 drinking glasses

What You Do

1. Place the raisins in the glass bowl.
2. Fill the bowl with water until it reaches about 1 inch (2.5 centimeters) above the raisins.
3. Cover the bowl with plastic wrap. Let the mixture sit in the refrigerator for two to three days. The longer you let it sit, the sweeter the drink becomes.
4. After two to three days, use a soup ladle to scoop the juice and raisins into two drinking glasses.

Makes 2 servings

CHAPTER 6

Laws, Rules, and Customs

Many other countries have ruled Afghanistan over the past 2,000 years. Each time a new group wins control, laws and rules in Afghanistan change.

In 2002, the country elected new leaders. They call their leaders the Loya Jirga, which means "assembly of chosen leaders." The Loya Jirga is a group who works to make decisions for the country. The Loya Jirga elected Hamid Karzai as the president of Afghanistan in June of 2002.

The Taliban

In the 1990s, a strict Muslim group called the Taliban took control of Afghanistan. Men were ordered to wear beards. Girls could not go to school. Women had to wear clothing that covered them from head to toe. The Taliban even ordered people to paint the windows on their houses. Women could not be seen from the street through the paint. The Taliban also outlawed playing with balloons and kites.

After the Taliban lost power in 2001, life changed for Afghan families. The Taliban had banned all TV and radio. People who had buried their TV sets in the yard dug them up. They also began reading magazines and listening to music again. People began selling colorful balloons and kites.

Members of the Loya Jirga make a decision by voting.

Afghanistan has had many flags over the years. After the Taliban lost power, the new leaders brought back a flag from 1962. The flag has three wide stripes of black, red, and green. An emblem in the middle shows a mosque, two flags, and wheat.

Afghanistan does not have any coins. In 2002, leaders issued new paper money. The paper money is called the afghani, or the new afghani. The bills are worth one, five, 10, 50, 500, or 1,000 afghanis.

Most Afghans are **Muslim**. Muslims follow the religion of Islam. They pray in buildings called **mosques**. Many Muslims pray five times a day.

Most Muslims celebrate Ramadan. Ramadan begins after the ninth new moon of the year, usually in October. Muslims fast, or go without eating, from dawn to dusk. Fasting helps remind each Muslim that poor, hungry people suffer every day. The month of Ramadan lasts until the next new moon.

Many school buildings were wrecked in wars. Sometimes children go to a neighbor's house for school. Others sit on the ground and have classes outdoors. Girls and boys often go to different schools.

Some children go to school in tents while they wait for their schools to be rebuilt.

String a Melon Seed Necklace

In Afghanistan, young children enjoy making jewelry out of everyday objects. They often string beads or seeds to make decorative neckwear. Melon seeds are a favorite choice. A single melon often has enough seeds to make an entire necklace.

What You Need

cantaloupe melon seeds (washed and dried)
length of dental floss, about 24 inches (60 centimeters)
sharp sewing needle
cork
scissors

What You Do

1. Thread the dental floss through the needle.
2. Tie a knot about 2 inches (5 centimeters) from the opposite end of the dental floss.
3. Lay a melon seed on the cork.
4. Press the needle through the melon seed.
5. Move the seed to the knot.
6. Continue steps 3 through 5 until the necklace is long enough to slip over your head.
7. Remove the needle and tie the two ends of the dental floss together with strong knots.
8. With scissors, trim the ends of the knotted dental floss.

CHAPTER 7

Pets in Afghanistan

The Afghan people love songbirds. Before the Taliban, many city families kept canaries and nightingales. During the years of Taliban rule, many people hid their birds.

Today, Afghans are once again buying and selling birds. Kabul has a market just for selling birds, grain, and birdcages. Children often work with their parents in the market to learn the business.

Many Afghans also keep pigeons. They like to watch the birds fly or even race. They train the pigeons to fly home to their cages.

At an Afghan market, a man offers a bird in a cage to buyers. Afghans enjoy keeping pet birds.

Afghan Hounds

English soldiers fighting in Afghanistan and India first saw Afghan hounds in the 1800s. Some soldiers brought these longhaired dogs back to England. Afghan hounds became prized pets. By the 1930s, some Afghan hounds had been brought to the United States.

Many families in Afghanistan allow their Afghan hounds to live outdoors. The dogs like to run in packs. They come home once a day for food. Families feed them wheat bread. The dogs also eat wild rabbits, fox, and deer.

CHAPTER 8

Sights to See in Afghanistan

Hundreds of white birds fill the area around the Blue Mosque in Mazar-e Sharif. Legends say that many of the birds are spirits. Legends also say that any gray birds at the mosque turn white after 40 days.

The Jaameh Mosque is the most famous site in Herat. Covered with blue tile, this mosque welcomes Muslims to prayer.

In Kabul, shops line Chicken Street. People sell bright carpets, jewels, birds, and glasswork. Buyers argue about prices with the sellers. Even after many wars, Chicken Street is a loud and colorful place.

Many white birds flock outside the Blue Mosque in Mazar-e Sharif.

Shoppers can buy colorful clothing and fabric from shops on Chicken Street in Kabul.

Glossary

cardamom (KAR-duh-muhm)—a spice made from the seeds of the cardamom plant

dung (DUHNG)—solid waste from animals used for fuel

mosque (MOSK)—a building used by Muslims for worship

Muslim (MUHZ-luhm)—a person who follows the religion of Islam; Islam is based on the teachings of the prophet Muhammad.

nomad (NOH-mad)—a person who travels from place to place to find food and water

pastry (PAY-stree)—a light, flaky sweet roll

Read More

Douglass, Susan L. *Ramadan.* On My Own Holidays. Minneapolis: Carolrhoda Books, 2004.

Fordyce, Deborah. *Welcome to Afghanistan.* Welcome to My Country. Milwaukee: Gareth Stevens, 2004.

Gunderson, Cory Gideon. *Afghanistan's Struggles.* World in Conflict: Middle East. Edina, Minn.: Abdo, 2003.

Useful Addresses

Afghan Community Foundation
P.O. Box 7870
Atlanta, GA 30357-0870

Embassy of Afghanistan
2341 Wyoming Avenue NW
Washington, DC 20036

Embassy of Afghanistan in Ottawa
246 Queen Street
Suite 400
Ottawa, ON K1P 5E4
Canada

Internet Sites

FactHound offers a safe, fun way to find Internet sites related to this book. All of the sites on FactHound have been researched by our staff.

Here's how:
1. Visit *www.facthound.com*
2. Type in this special code **0736824480** for age-appropriate sites.
   Or enter a search word related to this book for a more general search.
3. Click on the **Fetch It** button.

FactHound will fetch the best sites for you!

Index

Afghan hounds, 27
Amu River, 5

birds, 26, 28, 29
birthdays, 17
Blue Mosque, 28, 29
bread, 12, 20, 27. See also food

camels, 6, 14
celebrations, 16, 17, 24
Chicken Street, 28, 29
crops, 5, 12

desert, 6, 16
donkey, 12, 13
dung, 18, 19

family, 14, 17, 18, 20
farming, 10, 12
flag, 23
food, 12, 15, 20, 21

gems, 11
government, 22, 23

Herat, 28
highest point. See Nowshak
Hindu Kush Mountains, 4, 5
housing, 14

Jaameh Mosque, 28

Kabul, 5, 26, 28, 29
Kandahar, 14

Karzai, Hamid, 22
Khyber Pass, 4, 9

languages, 5
legend, 8, 10–11, 28
lowest point. See Amu River
Loya Jirga. See government

market, 12, 26
Mazar-e Sharif, 28, 29
money, 5, 23
mosque, 23, 24, 28

nomads, 14
Nowshak, 5

population, 5

Ramadan, 24
religion, 5, 24, 28. See also mosque

sandstorm, 16
school, 12, 24
season, 16, 17

Taliban, 22, 23, 26

villages, 12

wars, 14, 24
water, 13, 18
weather, 16, 21. See also sandstorms

SOUTH RUTLAND
ELEMENTARY LIBRARY